CAMPFIRE

PHILOSOPHY

Other books by Walt McLaughlin:

The Great Wild Silence
Ruminations and Excursions in the Adirondacks

A Reluctant Pantheism
Discovering the Divine in Nature

Cultivating the Wildness Within

The Impossible Cosmos
A Year of Amateur Astronomy and Big Questions

The Unexpected Trail
Taking on the 100 Mile Wilderness

Forest under my Fingernails
Reflections and Encounters on the Long Trail

The Allure of Deep Woods
Backpacking the Northville-Placid Trail

Arguing with the Wind
A Journey into the Alaskan Wilderness

Backcountry Excursions
Venturing into the Wild Regions of the Northeast

Loon Wisdom
Sounding the Depths of Wildness

Nature and Existence

Worldly Matters
Essays and Short Narratives

A Hungry Happiness

CAMPFIRE
PHILOSOPHY

Fragments from a Field Journal

Expanded Edition

by

Walt McLaughlin

Wood Thrush Books

Second Edition, Expanded

Published by Wood Thrush Books
           27 Maple Grove Estates
           Swanton, Vermont 05488

ISBN 978-1-7345175-1-4

Contents

Introduction

In 2006 I published *Campfire Philosophy* as a staple-stitched chapbook. The fragments in it were gleaned from a field journal kept between 1988 and 2003. My intention then was to share with readers some of the special moments I have experienced during various excursions into the wild – moments when I enjoyed flashes of insight that became the building blocks of a nature-based philosophy developed further in other publications of mine. I believed then, as I still do today, that these rough-edged yet candid fragments are easily digestible, therefore making this work a good introduction to my somewhat quirky worldview.

This is an expanded version of *Campfire Philosophy*. The text of the original chapbook has been reprinted in its entirety in the first section of this book. To that I have added a second installment of fragments extracted from a field journal kept between 2004 and 2017. No doubt an attentive reader will notice a significant shift in tone from the first section to the next. While my responses to the wild were largely emotional when I was younger, they have become more reflective in latter years. No surprise there, I suppose. Over time I have become comfortable with the wildness in both the world and myself, so now it's much easier to *think* about it.

In full disclosure, I must confess that I studied philosophy at Ohio University in the 1970s, and have read hundreds of philosophical works by a wide variety of thinkers since then, so I can't say that all my thoughts derive from direct encounters with the natural world. Yet wild places have been a constant source of inspiration to me, and my ventures into them have radically altered my worldview. I left academia as a religious existentialist, and have become something of a pantheist since then. That is not as unlikely a trajectory as one might think. In a rather insidious way, the wild answers the most profound questions that we pose during our deepest, most abstract cogitations.

On a more practical note, I should say a few things about the text itself. Culling excerpts from one's own journals is tricky business, indeed, as the temptation to rewrite the material while doing so is overwhelming. But something is often lost in the process. With this in mind, I have kept the lifted fragments as faithful to the original journal entries as possible, editing only for spelling and grammar, and changing a word here and there only to make it clear what exactly I was trying to say. In a few cases, the original journal entry was written in a kind of shorthand so words or phrases have been added in order to make sense of it. But for the most part, what I have copied over here is what was written in my field journals in the first place.

The month and year of these journal entries appear in the header, along with the place where they were written. Whenever a date is missing, the following entries were made in the same month and year stated in the previous heading. All the places mentioned in the headers are located in Vermont unless indicated otherwise. Sometimes I add a bit more information to the header, but don't like being too specific about my favorite haunts. After all, I still frequent many of these places and don't want to give them away.

Walt McLaughlin
January 2020

*I would have my thoughts, like wild apples, to be food
for walkers, and will not warrant them to be palatable
if tasted in the house.*

– Henry David Thoreau

CAMPFIRE

PHILOSOPHY

Field Journal
1988-2003

What a tenderfoot! I was off course a quarter mile last night. How I managed to drift off the trail, god only knows. I was tired and in a hurry and hiking in the twilight – that's all I can say in my defense. Still, no excuse. I wasn't in woods mode – that's all there is to it. Stumbling around in the woods like an idiot. Today I'm doing much better. It takes a while, but eventually I attune myself to my environment.

* * *

I took a dip in the brook then put on some nice clean clothes – what a concept! Feel almost civilized again. But there was a split second there, between the first dip in the water and the second, when I felt *completely* wild.

* * *

Sitting here by the brook, listening to the constant babble, I have a confession to make: I've been hearing Pan's flute for days now. At first I didn't want to deal with it, but there it is, loud and clear. And the rocks are singing… Hmm, only four days out and already hearing voices.

After eating a trout dinner, I sat back and sipped my coffee and thought about the ethics of fishing during spawning season. My conclusion: it's okay as long as you're careful and practice catch-and-release. So off I went, pole in hand, crisis resolved.

After about ten minutes of fishing, I hooked into a big trout. I hauled him in after a little play. With a fat, old, male tout in my hands, I hesitated. I shook with nervous joy as I dipped my hands alternately (to keep the trout wet), while struggling with the urge to keep him. Big old, fat male trout. Perhaps a full minute passed before I put him back in the water. He stayed in the middle of the pool, catching his breath in full view. A minute, perhaps two – who knows? – he and I looked at each other, then I tossed a pebble at him and he bolted to his favorite hiding spot.

* * *

Why do we have to work so hard to be happy? I wander the woods all day when I could be lounging around the house. Why? Because the clean air makes me feel so good? Because I need exercise? I don't know – I really don't. But even now as I scribble, I feel a certain sadness. Always, during every solo backpacking trip, there comes this moment. Sadness as a reprieve from so much happiness? The sadness of fatigue, perhaps? Or of solitude? No, something else – something to do with life itself. Out here, everything is stripped down to bare essentials. Even feelings.

Went over to that big, shallow pool shaded by boulders, took off my clothes, waded into the pool knee-deep, then freaked out. A snake on the rock! I quickly waded back out, dressed, then came back here to camp to fetch my binoculars. I was able to get within eight feet of the snake without spooking it. Studied it through the binoculars as it made its way up the rock. Two feet long, greenish-brown with a stripe running down its spine – pale white-yellow and a belly to match. Beautiful, actually. But I wasn't about to go back in that pool, even though I was sure it wasn't poisonous. Went to a different pool to dunk myself, thank you.

* * *

Spaced out big time while tending the fire this evening. Something akin to a hallucination. Was thinking about how I'm really more of a philosopher than a naturalist, then the brook protested. Spooky, very spooky. Maybe I should consider camping away from the brook next time. I've developed a bad habit of hearing things in that constant rush of water.

* * *

I deplore the cheap sentimentality of those who see Nature as all beauty and goodness – those who tell you that you shouldn't be fishing because it's cruel, as they don bug dope for a hike. Mosquitoes are just as much a part of the world as trout. Neither is any better or worse than me. We are all equal in God's eyes, I think: amoeba to man.

There is no good or bad in Nature. Mosquito, trout, man, even virus – it's all part of life, part of the continual struggle for existence. Things appear either good or bad from an anthropocentric viewpoint. God does not judge, man does. If I love Nature to its core, I must also love and respect its benign indifference. If I kill a mosquito with any more malice than I kill a trout, I am a hypocrite… too civilized for my own good.

* * *

The wild man is a willed man, as Thoreau says. Being half wild is being as free as you can be in this world. I am fortunate to have such freedom. I try to make the best of it. The most important thing is to not hurt yourself or others in the process of asserting your freedom. Easier said than done.

It's a queer feeling to crawl barefoot from a tent early in the morning with a loaded gun in hand. Went out to investigate all the noise in my camp. Turned out to be a few birds, that's all. I'm jumpy as hell right now. There are bear tracks and bear scat (pitch black, as in carnivore) all over this goddamned place. Coming from the airstrip to this spot along the river, I loudly cursed the fools who instructed me to say off game trails, especially bear trails. The bears own this place. They go wherever they want to go – wherever the Sitka spruce and/or alder bush is the least bit penetrable.

* * *

Had a visitor a half hour ago. A mother (ruffed?) grouse with two chicks in tow walked through my camp. I shot off a bunch of photos like a fool. She wouldn't let me get near enough for a close-up. The chicks successfully evaded me. Took maybe one half-decent photo, though, when I cut off their retreat. What a gas! With a loaded gun at my side, I could have feasted on grouse this evening easily. Not even a challenge. But I wouldn't do that. Fish only on this trip. Won't kill a bird or mammal unless I get into a survival situation. Besides, I think you need a license for that kind of bloodthirstyness. Nice visit. Come again.

* * *

Found the remains of two moose long since dead. One in the bush; the other near the river, complete with patches of bleached hair. Kept some teeth and ribs. Eerie. I see tracks, I see bones, but no live moose. I see bear tracks following moose tracks. It's a harsh world here in Alaska. Definitely not for the squeamish.

* * *

I got a little goofy as I came across the meadow this afternoon. I think I'm a little bushed already. It *has* been a while since I last saw or talked to anyone. I guess it only stands to reason. The more comfortable I become here, the bushier I get. Seems like I get distracted a lot easier now, too. I spend a great deal of time watching the birds through my binoculars, especially bald eagles. I check them out several times a day. Can't get used to them. They're such magnificent birds. I'd like to see one go in for a kill – catch a salmon or another bird or something. They do an awful lot of waiting around, looking for an opportunity.

* * *

What to do with the trout? Now here's a brand new puzzle. I never dreamt that I would have to consider *not* eating the trout that I caught here, but then the reality of brown bears is quite different from the theory. I'm really not crazy about attracting attention to myself. Clothes reeking of cooked trout would be the equivalent of inviting brown bear to dinner. I've seen one brownie, thank you. I think that's enough.

* * *

I've spent too much time trying to figure out why the world is the way it is and not enough time living in it. A part of me has always held back, as if waiting for the final piece of the puzzle to fall into place before passing judgment on the world and taking hold of it with both hands. No more, no more, no more – this very moment. I am here to live in the world, not pass judgment on it.

* * *

This is why I came alone to Alaska: I needed a drastic measure to shake me lose from the stranglehold of existential paralysis. By god it's working! I am living each day to its fullest now. If I leave this wilderness alive, I'll continue doing so. I will stop bitching about the world and change it if need be, however I can. If I can survive out here, then I'm not *entirely* impotent. So on with it then. On with life and to hell with all this

20

whimpering about what we can and cannot know. No more paralysis – anything but that!

* * *

Fire, water, earth and sky – these are the things that concern me now. An elemental existence. There are animals and vegetation as well, of course. That's about it. What I brought with me: steel, plastic, woven fibers. And a few chemicals. It's remarkable how much of my gear is unnatural, which is to say, manmade. So much of civilized life is divorced from the natural world.

* * *

Heard the unmistakable howl of a lone wolf miles away, deep in the Endicott Wilderness. Bone chilling. Exactly what I didn't expect to hear while looking at flowers. Fear and loneliness returned in a flash. The bush is so quiet right now. I could have been mistaken. Maybe I didn't hear a wolf howling. Maybe I don't want to hear it.

* * *

Jesus, I can't believe it. Momma bear and her two cubs just walked through my camp like I was no big deal at all – feeding on roots all the way, sniffing around my wash basin and occasionally get up on their hind legs to check me out. Right past me, one slow step at a time, south to north, from the river to the woods, towards the airstrip. I had my gun out, I had my bear repellant out, but what for? I put them away, then went into my tent to fish out my camera and take another picture of them. This is really too much. What the hell is going on here? I don't know what to think. Would like to invite them for dinner. They're all looking pretty lean. Definitely a hump on Momma's back, though. Jesus, I don't even know if I should be afraid any more or not. They act like they don't give a damn about me. Why be afraid? Cautious, certainly – *don't* invite them for dinner, but what? I don't know. In all the bear stories I read and heard, nothing prepared me for this. It feels like all I can do is keep a respectful distance and stay on the look out. I've two more days in the bush…

Lured by the sun on a chilly yet cloudless day, I have come to this fine, south-facing ledge on the pretense of flower hunting and bird watching. Saw a pair of cardinals down by the railroad tracks, not far away. Also saw hepatica, spring beauty, and Dutchman's breeches in full bloom. But now as I sit here, with Giant Mountain over Shelburne Point and Mt. Philo due south across the bay, I realize that I've come here for a reason that goes beyond words, beyond my amateur science.

* * *

Contemplation never comes easy – not even in the lap of nature. I try too hard. I think too much or not enough. The important things, seemingly unimportant in the time-bound routine of daily life, can easily slip past if I am not watchful. Even scribbling in this notebook, I jeopardize my chance to catch it.

Dusk. Boiling up water by campfire. Saving stove fuel since the wood is so dry. Just finished roasting the trout. Caught four more, kept two, for a total of three for dinner since I still had one from this afternoon. Tasty. Hit the spot. But three was enough since two of them were nine inches long and had some meat on them.

The peepers in the lower pond are making a racket, but they'll shut up soon. They've been peeping off and on all evening. Can't make up their minds. A thrush sang for a while; an owl hooted. But the woodpeckers are the real entertainment here. They cry out, knock loudly, chase each other around. I watched two of them fall to the ground – thought maybe it was an injured bird until two birds, male and female, flew away. It's that time of year.

I do not wish to applaud the glories of nature and sneer at the miserable constructs of man. It's wrong, I think, to hide behind nature, use her as a mere shield while throwing stones at humanity. Stones I have many – I showed Judy a few last night. But what is best about nature is that she does not judge, she does not moralize. She goes about her brute business with little concern for how it might be interpreted. Can I philosophize without moralizing? If not, then I should keep my mouth shut. The world has enough preachers.

I think a trout hit my bait earlier this evening – a remarkable feat considering the status of the brook: murky torrent full of whitewater, with patches of snow along its banks. Trying to fish this early in the season is a true exercise in futility. But what the heck… it's more spring rite than actual sport.

Wood nice and dry so dinner went very smoothly. Lingered by the fire afterward but no profound thoughts, no real introspection. Full moon rising into partly cloudy sky – a true wonder to behold. Temps still remarkably mild. Nice and toasty in dry clothes. Was a true joy to get my wet boots and socks off. I'm sure that I'll sleep well tonight.

I just had an incredible fishing experience. Left the North Lamoille and drove here early afternoon. Walked down to a familiar hole on the Seymour River and caught two rather large brook trout. Wasn't all that surprised. I've done well at that hole before, when wildflowers were in bloom. Many flowers out today, including trout lily, trillium, violets, wood anemone, spring beauty and Dutchman's breeches. The difference between here and the North Lamoille is elevation, I think – about 500 to 1,000 feet. Anyhow, I continued up the Seymour River to a spot where I'd caught a rainbow trout many years ago. The land around the hole was posted with no trespassing signs, but I waded up the stream, mid-thigh, since that's legal. Last time I was here, people in the nearby house unleashed a vicious dog on me. No dog this time. The hole was incredible! Caught five large rainbows in a half hour. Departed with them like a bandit.

I spent a lot of time on top of Bone Mountain, looking around and meditating. I don't want to go into the details of the meditation, not even here. It suffices to say that I've reestablished contact with my Maker and restructured my thinking so that the most important things come first. So easy to forget what's important. The mind remembers but the heart forgets. That's why a trip like this is crucial.

* * *

The Bone hike was challenging, but left me with enough energy to putter about camp effortlessly. I've slackened my pace, too, so now I'm more in rhythm with my surroundings. And my camp along the Pinneo is beginning to feel like home away from home. Only the cold air is daunting, but I intend to remedy that soon with a sustained fire.

Movement – this is a new experience for me. I'm used to sitting and thinking. Not too much thinking going on lately. Today's thought: backpacking is a bourgeois invention. That isn't meant to be critical, but I suppose it is. Only privileged people can invest so much time and energy into frivolous activity. Same as writing or the arts, in that respect.

* * *

I haven't decided yet whether movement is a good thing or not. There's no denying the recreational value of backpacking or hiking: fresh air, exercise, and all that. But is movement – constant movement – good for the soul? Or is it better to simply sit still and pay attention? I am awed by the changes in the landscape as I move. Nature has another surprise waiting for me right around the next turn in the trail. It is difficult to hike and *not* feel joyous. But at the same time, I often catch myself daydreaming. After a while, I feel like I'm in some netherworld – entranced by the green infinity through which I pass. Only a vista, beaver pond, roaring brook or sudden sound snaps me out of it. But in no time, I'm in the green again… intoxicated completely. Today, for example, I stopped to prod a toad from the trail with my walking stick, saying: "Mister Toad. Big, fat and slow

Mister Toad. Good thing you're wearing camo!" How come I've never encountered anything like that in a treatise on nature? It's almost as if the most important thing we experience in the wild is a secret.

* * *

Worst thing about campfires is that they slow me down. *Best* thing is that they slow me down. It's not good to be in too much of a rush out here.

* * *

The forest is under my fingernails. A mountain stream runs through me. I smell of sweat, rotting duff, and wood smoke. I am no less wary than a fleeting deer or chipmunk. Several weeks now without TV, newspaper or radio, I feel as if I actually belong in this green world, as if Creation was a good idea. The wind sweeps across my brow. I've given enough blood to insects to feel like a part of the plan. My feet follow an unending trail lined with bunchberry and yellow lilies, but my spirit soars high overhead, amid the clouds. In these home woods, I'm slowly sinking my heart deep into gray bedrock, never to be removed. My progress north is painstakingly slow today. And that is as it should be – a celebration of simple, earthy joy, lacking all pretense.

30

Easy descent down an old logging road partly overgrown with timothy. Preston Brook within earshot; Robbins Mountain looming overhead. Summer in bloom along the track: bracken, dewberry, purple flowering raspberry, clover, vetch, hawkweed and even daisies. Temps almost perfect. Birds singing. I feel so incredibly lucky to be here, to be healthy and alive!

*   *   *

Eternity is now. The planet swirls endlessly with growth and decay. The stars and galaxies come and go forever. Nature is but a manifestation of God. He who loves the wildflower opening in early morning, woodpecker knocking at midday, or a thrush singing at dusk is already saved. Salvation is life celebrated with each deep breath drawn; damnation is that numbness to the world arising from a fixation with profit and loss. Heaven unfolds daily. The resurrection is an ongoing affair. There is no past, present or future in God's heart. Nor should there be in ours. The wild is all there is of any true significance. We have a moral duty to revel in it.

*   *   *

To gaze across familiar mountains and valleys on a glorious summer day and call this beautiful place "home" over and over, is to celebrate the profound yet simple joy of merely being alive. I *still* don't give a damn about the big brag of end-to-end, not really, but it has been an excellent opportunity to see the Green Mountains, to live in them as if their rock and my bones were one in the same. I *still* can't get over my great good fortune, just being able to do this – hike for a month in the beautiful mountainous forest in my back yard.

* * *

God, humankind and nature are inexorably entwined. Inseparable. There is no sense speaking of one without speaking of the other two.

* * *

God is the ultimate paradox: order out of chaos. God is the driving force of the universe – the Urge that loosely binds all things, both physical and spiritual, animate and inanimate, together in a fabric of time and space.

* * *

Nature is all things, ordered and unordered, in the universe. Nature is both balance and disjointedness – order *and* chaos.

32

Humankind can either live in accordance with God/nature, or against it. That is its ultimate *moral* choice.

33

* * *

Voices from the wilderness: as long as humankind still has *some* link to the natural world, all is not lost – there is reason to hope.

Went fly fishing early evening, catching three brookies (one nine-inch trout on a Light Cahill and two six-inchers on an Ausable Wulff). Cooked up the big one with dinner. Judy ate it with some reluctance when she found out it was a female (sisterhood is powerful). Looks like I'll be doing catch-and-release today.

* * *

Judy and I hung out in a deep pool about a hundred yards below camp, after a long sweaty hike up to Lye Brook Falls and back. Cooled off nicely, then made love on the rocks. It doesn't get any better than this. Am thinking about going fishing but lack the ambition. We'll see what the skies do first.

* * *

Funny how quickly we forget how pleasant it is just to sit quietly in these woods. A couple of hours from now, we'll be in the bustle of Manchester – less than that, actually. And all this will be but a memory until next time. I wish, for Judy's sake, we could stay out here another day. Maybe next year.

Evening alone in the cool, wet forest. After an hour of unproductive fly-casting, I am asking that age-old question: Do fish exist? The stream is running high and fast – not as bad as the streams flowing into the Lamoille River to the north, but bad enough to keep the trout under cover. I'm angry with myself for not getting a legitimate weather report before coming out here. As far as the fishing goes, this is an utter waste of time. But then I remember that just being here is the main thing. The air smells incredibly fresh. Everything around me is lush. It is good to be here, fish or no fish.

Late evening. Put out my campfire and retired into the tent as soon as darkness settled in. My German shepherd dog, Jesse, is a nervous wreck. Hasn't cracked a smile since we returned from a short bout of fishing. I think it has finally dawned on her that we're spending the night here – her first overnighter in the woods. She's all eyes and ears (not to mention nose), looking out the screen door for critters… or maybe the boogeyman. I think it's going to be a long night.

Jesse sees her first moose, at a beaver pond deep in the wilderness. She's ears up and nose down for the next half hour. Can't get that smile off her face.

Late morning. Just back from an hour-long hike around the pond with Jesse. Waves of frogs parting before us. Blue jay feathers. Signs of beaver activity. Abandoned, busted-out skiff. Meadowsweet, jewelweed, wintergreen and Indian pipe in bloom. Dried up feeder streams. Shallow, muddy water along shoreline (the shelter surrounded by prime real estate as far as fishing and swimming goes). Mature forest – hasn't been cut in a long while. A few beaver paths down to the water but no trail around the pond. Jesse gets a good workout. So do I.

* * *

Judy, Jesse and I swam out to a rock in the pond around noon, just before eating lunch. Nice swim. Surprised that Jesse went all the way out there and back with us. Just goes to show the power of bonding. We're her pack now.

* * *

Loon on the pond, diving for fish. Call loudly echoing into the wind.

A waning moon on the rise last night, brightening the place. Bullfrogs made such a racket it was hard to sleep. Pond remains mysteriously still all morning. Another partly cloudy sky. And birds chirping. A bit of breeze in the trees; the low hum of a skidder in the distance – maybe three miles away. Airplane. Frog splash jumping sound. Pervasive forest quiet. It's a good day to do nothing, nothing at all.

Only a few hours in the woods and already I'm feeling more relaxed than I've felt in months. It never ceases to amaze me how quickly the wild can unravel my nerves. Being alone helps. With no one to talk to, I'm less inclined to drag all my mental baggage out here. Just me, my dog, the woods, the sun and the stream.

Dusk came quickly. No sooner did I clean up the dishes and the day was over. Burned a "sacrifice" copy of my Long Trail book, then called it a night. Making this entry with the last bit of energy I have. Jesse has already crashed. Correction: she's waiting patiently for me to put out the light.

* * *

Awe, gratitude, joy. How else to wander through these woods? A sense of reverence. Each step the bushwhacker takes should be a prayer. God is the wild.

* * *

Remnant words on ashen paper that disintegrates when I touch it – humbling, indeed. Words do not endure. Into the charcoal soup they go – all my words – until only the cold, black patch of a dismantled campfire remains. Now only so much fertilizer for trilliums. My footprints vanish with time. So do my words. Wordsmith or bushwhacker, it is all the same.

Knocked a tiger swallowtail butterfly out of the air and into the brook with my fly rod – a freak accident. Helpless in the cascading water, it was sure to drown. So I ran downstream, fished it out of the drink, then put it on my shoulder. There it stayed during the next five to ten minutes of fishing, until its wings dried out enough for it to fly away. A delightful encounter – perhaps more for me than the butterfly.

Waterthrush serenading me at dawn – the same bird I heard last night, misnamed because I wasn't really paying attention, wasn't fully here yet. So it goes. You can get into the woods in a minute, but it takes a day for the woods to get into you.

I do love the woods. Can't imagine being happy without a nearby forest in which to roam. On this count, I'm sure my dog would agree, though she seems to be better, much better, than me at finding happiness wherever she goes.

Campfire kept me company until the full moon rose last night, about an hour after dark. Owl hooting in the distance. Jesse grooving on night sounds that I can't even hear. A sense of desolation came over me while I was fishing, but dissipated the moment I had the fire going. It's like that. A campfire is good company. So is the moon, whose light is softer than the sun's.

* * *

The world has scientists aplenty to describe nature and environmentalists by the busload to fight for it. But who speaks for nature as if both God and man were an integral part of it?

* * *

While I speculate, Jesse chases a local up a hemlock tree. The terrorized squirrel directly in front of me, about fifteen feet up, vocalizes its distress. Now the whole neighborhood is upset. Ears up and looking around, Jesse sits down amid dry leaves, looking for further evidence of her distant past. She and I are very much alike that way.

The treetops across the brook are illuminated by sunrise, but I'm still in the shadows here in the ravine. No matter. The surrounding woods are aflame with autumnal color and the sky overhead is blue. Sipping coffee as I snuggle around a campfire, staving off the morning chill. Jesse, on guard all night, is finally sleeping. The brook roars, otherwise all is quiet. Coyotes yelping just before daybreak, otherwise it was a quiet night, with the dark sky overhead full of stars. I slept well – best night's sleep I've had in a long time – so today I'm feeling ready for anything. As soon as my diminishing pile of wood is gone, I'll break camp and hike out. But for now, this delicious forest and healing calm.

Campfire philosophy: thoughts that can withstand the unblinking gaze of the flame. This is no time for bullshit or abstraction. Keep it real, very real.

* * *

Went down to the lake's edge after dinner to try my luck with the fly rod during the last hour of yesterday's light. Loons fishing just offshore – a good omen. Trout rising to a light mayfly hatch. I threw a #18 Adams out there and a brookie jumped out of the water for it. Brought him to the shoreline, then lost him. A few other hits after that, but no trout landed. I fly-fished until the bats came out. Changed my fly one last time, in the dark, by flashlight. A good time, even if I did walk away empty-handed.

* * *

Wilderness Areas are refuges for our wilder selves. When they no longer exist, we will cease to be fully human.

* * *

It is so quiet that I make up cricket sounds to fill the void. Occasional buzzing mosquito. Leaves rustling. And then the thump of hooves or paws not far away. A few songbirds in the distance. The air now perfectly still… Patches of azure blue in the somber green forest at dusk. Chipmunks on the forest floor. A drone in the distance, very low. Is that the sound of civilization?

* * *

Wood thrush barely audible – no louder than the fire. My whole life is but an attempt to do justice to that bird's song, deep in the forest. Its song is the earth rejoicing. A forest hymn.

* * *

The difference between illusion and reality is perception. This is what the wild teaches us.

* * *

Waiting for the wild to dispense its little nuggets of wisdom, like a fisherman waiting for the trout to rise…

* * *

A water spider makes itself look like a stick when it's threatened. The genius of nature, inspired by survival.

The reeds bend without hesitation to the steady southwest breeze. Such is the relationship between nature and God… making it impossible, at times, to tell the difference between the two.

* * *

Utter chaos is a human contrivance.

Whoa! Right at my feet, emerging from the forest duff, a queen bee still groggy from her winter nap. She stumbles towards me; doesn't seem to be with the program yet. I step aside, making way for Her Highness.

* * *

I don't so much love nature as feel at home in it. I'm more of an admirer than a lover of nature, really. The wild is too harsh sometimes to suit me.

* * *

What astonishes more, nature's simplicity or its complexity? Looking about, I'm amazed by the richness and diversity on this small hill. And yet elementally speaking – earth, rock, tree, flower – it's all pretty basic. Simple yet beautiful, like the mosaic that lichen and moss make on the side of a boulder. Okay, maybe I'm more of a nature lover than I admit. But beauty still doesn't impress me as much as the sublime. The wild has teeth to it and that's what I admire about it most.

I followed the brook past the last sap line, stumbling into a logging yard shut down for mud season. Crisscrossing the brook, following an abandoned skidder trail, I climbed higher in the valley, deeper into the woods, for about a half hour. Sun amid clouds burned through the leafless trees, heating me right up. I kept climbing, wondering why I was doing so, until I came to a single painted trillium – my favorite flower – only inches high and days old. I climbed no higher, dropping down to a small pool to cool out. On my hands and knees, dunking my head, I lapped up several gulps of ice-cold water. The headwall, less than a mile away, rose so sharply that I knew there were no beavers or humans above me. A simple, primordial pleasure – reason enough to come here.

Sterling Pond

What I love most about this pond is its intense silence – like now – when the wind dies down and the people are gone. Stillness and silence – as close to God as you can get, some say. Conifers motionless on the opposite shore. There now, a jet in the distance and a bird chirping – no idea who. Flies buzzing and the occasional *plop* of a rising trout. This place screams the wild. Four ravens in the thermals, circling the sun. Gust of wind. So easy to spend all day on this pond. I rediscover my wilder self every time I come here. It can't be helped.

I've backed away from the falls fifty yards or so, in order to hear myself think. The roar of the falls is mesmerizing – good for clearing the head, bad for contemplation.

* * *

Hidden beauty. How far will one go to find it? How much gets overlooked?

* * *

The pursuit of beauty and the pursuit of divine revelation may spring from the same desire, the same source, the same sense of *joie de vivre*. That would explain our attraction to the sublime.

* * *

How much water has flowed past while I've been sitting here? More riddle than science, the answer is not a matter of time or quantity. It's the riddle of living, of being aware.

I didn't bring my rod today. The roily brook tells me that that's probably for the best. Just saw a mayfly in the air (a sulphur dun?), but fishing couldn't be too good right now. No matter. I'm not in the mood for it, anyhow. I'm in the mood to sweat, to do some miles, to let my thoughts mingle with the eternal green all around me.

* * *

Out here, solitude is unequivocal, intense, even if you occasionally pass someone on the trail. Home is a comfortable solitude, too "inner" to be of much use.

* * *

No matter how happy I am, no matter how beautiful the day is in this great outdoors, I am never far from the fundamentally existential sadness that comes with an acute awareness of life/death – the juxtaposition that *all* living things face. Joy and sadness are flip sides of the same coin, to be sure.

Trespassing.   When tomorrow's rain washes away my tracks, the farmer who owns this land won't know that I've been here. I move through the woods like a ghost, interested more in the wild itself than his meager attempt to possess it.

On a mountaintop like this, alone, one can't help but feel like a king or one of the immortals. I've lost ten years since the trailhead, at least. Like the gods on Olympus, I look down upon the world, feeling somewhat detached from all worldly cares. And proud of myself for making it up here. An acceptable hubris?

Caught up with a thru hiker, Snail Male, who's on the last leg of his LT hike end-to-end. Out here celebrating his 50th birthday. Tall, thin, good-humored fellow with thinning hair and a nearly white beard. Discouraged by all the rain. Hasn't had a decent view since Stark's Nest. But in the absence of photos, he's keeping a detailed journal of his trip. Told him that I did the same and ended up writing a book about the journey. Turns out he's read the book. We're both surprised.

* * *

Just before parting, Snale Male showed me his chicken-in-the-woods – a slab of tree mushroom the size of my hand, bright orange on top and pale yellow on bottom. He's going to have it with his ramen noodles tonight. Snail Male knows his 'shrooms, "This one's a delicacy," he says. I wouldn't risk it… but I do envy him his natural fête this evening.

Owl hooting just after dark; lone coyote crying out in the middle of the night.   Rain now at daybreak. Warm night – never zipped up my sleeping bag. Slept well beneath the tarp, caressed by a gentle breeze. Incredible stillness at midnight, though, making a single mosquito sound a thousand times louder than it is.

* * *

Around me on the ground, hundreds of thumb-sized cones playing nature's game of chance. Which one will become a fir tree like those overhead?   It hardly matters. All is dust, eventually. Life is as ephemeral as the rain.

Field Journal
2004-2017

Midmorning Monday. Sitting near my favorite rocky overhang on this brook, on a sunny summer day. Sweaty from the short hike in here – humid woods. Haze in the sunny openings along the brook. Everything's damp… but the air temperature is just about perfect for sitting here. Have found a comfortable place along the rocky bank to sit and think. No rod today; just me and my thoughts. Woke up in the middle of the night last night with a powerful insight into my literary life. Figure this is the right place to follow that train of thought. Better get to it.

* * *

To write courageously – that's the issue here.

* * *

Why can't I accept the fact that I'm as much a philosopher as I am a woodsman or writer?   It's not like I have a choice – I can't just give it up. My happiness and deeper sense of well being are tied to this three-pronged identity.

* * *

The mayflies have stopped coming off the water. The reflection off the rippling stream has crept up the shadowy overhang as the sun has shifted higher into the sky. Mosquitoes are getting after me now, for some reason. It's time to go. I have enough ideas to take home with me. It's almost lunchtime. I'll enjoy the hike out.

Midday at a small, active beaver pond (100 feet across) just below Smuggler's Notch. Followed the stream from where it crosses the road a couple miles north of here. Rough going – hobblebush country. Game trails pointing the way, though. Followed them here, to the edge of the spring season, a couple hundred feet below where Route 108 makes a final swing before entering the Notch. Have seen these beaver ponds from the road many times. At long last, I've come here.

The main pond – maybe an acre or two – has recently drained. But this smaller pond is doing just fine. A little vegetation on the dam but fresh sticks on the lodge. Beavers still live here. Between this pond and the headwall, a few more puddles trying to be ponds, but this is obviously the main event. Fish rising here to midges. I've tossed my smallest fly over the water only to have it denied. Feeding is lackluster, actually. It's overcast, chilly (temps around 50 degrees), with a bit of wind. More like late April than late May. Above the pond, the northern ridge of Mt. Mansfield is still speckled with snow. The vernal line maybe 200 or 300 feet above me. It's early spring here and the peepers revel in it, as do the trilliums and trout lilies.

I came here for the quiet wildness of this place and haven't been disappointed. But I can't stay much longer. Tramping these wetlands, I'm wet up to my knees and feeling the chill. Will have to get moving shortly. Maybe I can find another beaver pond farther downstream. Might have missed one.

* * *

Indeed, I found another beaver pond farther downstream and caught an eight-inch brookie on the first cast! Followed that with a dozen smaller ones as the sun slid in and out of the clouds and a light mayfly hatch developed. Go figure.

Came here to spend the night and cast off a pissy mood. Came here on orders from Judy. Doubt 24 hours here will make much difference in my outlook, but I welcome the opportunity to be alone in the woods for a while and relax. I feel a nap coming on. After that, who knows? Intentionally didn't bring my fly rod. Not in that kind of mood. Would rather sit and think. Or whatever.

* * *

Owls in the middle of the night. A barred owl and something else. The sounds of darkness.

* * *

Slight breeze and the forest is dancing. Narcotic effect. I feel like dancing with it.

* * *

What is important; what is not? This is a life and death issue. I'd hate to wake up when I'm 80 and suddenly realize that most of my days were wasted.

Camped at my favorite site along this brook, just below Kaylee and Judy's swimming hole. Jesse's ashes (half of them, that is) are buried at the base of a tree about ten feet away. Her memory is keeping me company this evening. I sunk another dry fly into a young tree here to deepen the personal mythos of the place. I intend to return here for many hears to come, adding layer upon layer of memories. As old haunts go, this one is the most haunted. Might as well keep it that way.

* * *

Coffee and a campfire on a sunny morning in the mountains and life is good. Slept fairly well last night even though my points of contact with the ground – hips, shoulders, etc. – were all sore when I got out of bed. Awoke a couple times in the middle of the night and just lied there staring at the multitudes of stars sparkling through the forest canopy. Quite the night. Caught a slight chill at one point, but it passed (temps never below 40 degrees). Now it's a picture perfect day with beams of sunlight illuminating the upper reaches of the yellow/green forest. Couldn't ask for more.

Shortly after leaving Silver Lake, I heard a tree fall. A couple minutes later, I found a freshly downed hemlock. If a tree falls in the forest and I hear it, should I be worried?

* * *

Pondering Emerson while strolling through ambient woods, approaching Sacandaga River. "A walk in the woods is only an exalted dream," he said. A heavy pack changes things a tad, but for the most part I concur.

* * *

Mushrooms are a good example of nature's diversity and strangeness.

* * *

Gear versus skill. One is acquired with the outlay of cash; the other requires learning.

* * *

There is no good reason for taking the punishment of the trail. Lured by the wild, I make up excuses for being here.

* * *

Gurgling, growling stomach, complaining that it's not getting enough to eat. I keep myself adequately fueled for the journey. That is all. It's a kind of forest asceticism – a thru-hiker rejection of eating for eating's sake. I move better on a nearly empty stomach.

* * *

Saw the first unmistakable sign of bear activity back at Bloodgood Brook (claw marks on beech trees) and am too deep in the woods to resupply. I've never lost food to bears before, but there's always a first time. Hope that first time isn't tonight.

* * *

Awoke this morning to the chattering of squirrels. Looked over and saw my food bags dangling in the trees, thinking I'm good to go. That was my second thought, actually. My first thought was a phrase uttered by the French philosopher Alain: "The life of the woods is a fiction; the man of the woods is a fugitive." I have been haunted by that phrase for years, even though it

68

would be easy to dismiss it as the haughty notion of an effete intellectual sitting in a Parisian café. I too have sat in the center of the civilized world and felt its power, wondering what drives me into these woods in such hot pursuit of grubby experience. Am I a pilgrim on a spiritual quest or merely a social misfit running away from complexities I neither like nor understand? A godless man, Alain ruled out the possibility of the former. So what is left?

I had a powerfully erotic dream last night, snuggled up to a gaggle of beautiful, young women in some bistro in an unnamed French city, eating, drinking and being merry in general. I awoke to a forest washed in moonlight, a deep chill and terrible silence. Naturally, I got up to pee, then went back to bed to sleep some more. But now, at daybreak, I wonder what truly motivates me. Hard to say. All I know is that there is running to and running from, and today I'm running directly to West Lake, the heart of this wilderness, to spend some time and harvest an intangible joy that guys like Alain could never hope to understand. It cuts both ways, no doubt.

* * *

Wow. What a feeling to be standing on a rock in the middle of a lake, in the middle of nowhere, casting a fly while loons are calling and the sun is setting. Then absolutely no sound. So quiet here that a passing woodpecker scared the crap out of me. No rise, but who cares?

• • •

Thinking while staying put is reflective. Thinking while moving is more like a daydream.

* * *

"Luck is a rogue force that prevents human life from being fully domesticated to rational management," said Nicholas Rescher in his book on the subject. You can say that again. As I write this, clouds thicken and the wind picks up. Is that thunder in the distance? I'd better get going.

* * *

Traveling like a turtle, with a house on my back.

* * *

Miller Falls. Beautiful. A photograph doesn't do it justice. All of a sudden, I realize that I have to enrich my life with more beauty and the celebration of it. In a nutshell: art, music, poetry and prayer.

* * *

Had lunch on the small grassy knoll (just beyond Ouluska Stream) where John Rondeau had his hermitage. That was very cool. To be sure, the man was in the middle of nowhere. Picked his site well, though. I couldn't have done better.

* * *

You know you're the first one through when there are spider webs across the trail.

* * *

Sky full of stars just past midnight, when I went out to pee. Saw Cassiopeia and Cygnus in the Milky Way, the Great Square of Pegasus overhead, and even the hint of Andromeda Galaxy at zenith. Pleiades seem closer than usual. Taurus. A sky full of heavenly bodies. Beautiful. Glad I didn't have my binoculars, otherwise I would've caught a chill looking around.

* * *

Slipped and fell off greasy puncheon – a soft landing in the moss.

* * *

71

Trail became gnarly as soon as it left Duck Hole. Wet woods, too, so the understory soaked me good. Set of large deer tracks got my attention, then a set of bear tracks – I counted the toes. That was along Roaring Brook (an attractive stream to fish). Lost the tracks by the time I reached the notch between Roaring Brook and the Moose Creek drainage. *Very* wild there and I started grooving on it. Yessir, I found a wilder self in deep woods, once again.

Trail became even more gnarly as it dropped down towards Moose Creek. Skirted a series of new beaver ponds drowning the trail. Crossed a beaver dam at one point. Stopped to admire a new beaver lodge at another, then took a stick from the dam – my new walking stick. Negotiated the rest of the Moose Creek wetlands with it, thus transforming from a trekker to a woodswalker.

* * *

Wherever you build a campfire, that's home for the night. A warm feeling, even if it's a dismal place.

* * *

Funny, I can't tell the difference between the dankness of the forest and the dankness of my gear. I guess the forest has consumed me. That's a good thing.

Late afternoon. Camp set up now. Snacking on a granola bar and nuts while writing this, washing it all down with cold water just pumped from the brook. Matika nearby, chewing on a stick. She's not quite sure what to make of all this. Doesn't know what the tent is or why we're not heading back home. She'll find out soon enough. Not a worrier like my old dog, Jesse, Matika is happy enough just chewing her stick.

* * *

Caddis fly on my belly, perfectly content there. Good sign. I'll break out my rod and do a little fly casting soon. Someone might rise to it.

* * *

Caught my first brook trout of the year while fly-fishing this afternoon. Matika stunned when I put the trout in her face. I dropped it in the shallow water at her feet and she was five minutes looking for a creature that was gone the second it hit the water. It's amazing what she doesn't know.

* * *

Will probably do a little fly-fishing later this morning, if only to stay out here a bit longer. Am in no hurry to break camp and go back to town. Suddenly it occurs to me that everything back there can wait. *This* is more important. If I do nothing else the rest of my life, I hope to somehow convey this fact. How terribly easy it is to lose perspective.

What was a middling mood that could have gone either way is becoming a good one as the forest clears away my stinky thoughts. I anticipate a pleasant walk back to the car, full of daydreams. Just hope it doesn't go by too quickly.

Deep woods. Only two miles from the trailhead; might as well be twenty. Haven't seen as much as a boot print since that first hour hiking in here. Oddly enough, this clearing has more human detritus than can be found anywhere else: a glass bottle here, a piece of rusty old metal strapping there. This forest is living up to its name – a wilderness to be sure. Crickets all around us. Gusts of wind. The occasional chirp. Otherwise an intense quiet. I can hear the trickle of the stream 200 feet away. I can hear myself breathing. Am getting what I came for, no doubt.

Matika is jumpy. She's having her first wilderness experience. It's about time. As for me, well, I can feel myself unraveling.

* * *

Regarding nature and existence (an ongoing meditation): the world is neither rational nor irrational. Both reason and absurdity are human.

* * *

Thoreau was right: indoor thoughts are quite different from outdoor ones. And those in deep woods are in a category of their own.

* * *

Discipline issues. Young Matika, with more energy than sense, wants to dart after every critter moving across the forest floor. Between that and getting into burs, she's a distraction. On the other hand, this is an ideal environment for teaching obedience. Instinctively she knows better than to get too far away from me.

* * *

Tuesday afternoon. Just finished a late lunch. Hard to believe I've been here 24 hours already. I think I've finally kicked back to wilderness time. The bushwhack upstream today was effortless, yet I was gone an hour and a half. Go figure.

* * *

Funny how much more friendly these woods seem, now that I know the lay of the land.

* * *

The only difference between a billow smoke, a cloud and a nebula is scale. This leads me to believe that the better part of existence is ephemeral.

* * *

I suppose it is indicative of my species, that I find it difficult to stay in one place very long without radically altering my environment.

* * *

I do not fully understand the wild's hold on me. All I know is that without it I would perish.

• • •

Tuesday evening. Early dinner this evening and I've banked the cooking coals until I'm ready for a campfire meditation. Coming soon. But first a little attention given to the sights and sounds of the forest at dusk. Subtle indeed. It is easy to miss them. If I listen carefully, I can hear the highway traffic miles away – for better or worse. Not deep enough in the woods to miss that. But I don't mind it too much. It's far enough away to be rather insignificant. A single bird chirping. Crickets and the trickle of water; the yellowing leaves of the birch overhead, a few wispy clouds and tall grass undulating in a barely discernable wind. The smell of the forest, the campfire and myself all mixed together. A chill in the air warning of a very cool night ahead (I'm already wearing my wool shirt). A strange mechanical sound coming from the south, too many miles away to identify. Can't even venture a guess what it is. Ah well… This is why I usually camp close to the brook. Could just be the sound of highway traffic distorted by the mountains.

* * *

A writer has less direct power than he or she expects, and more indirect power than he or she realizes.

* * *

Words, words, words. The world cannot be saved by words alone… but it can be coaxed in the right direction by them. The trick is to know when to stop talking and take action.

* * *

Illustrate the example. By writing about these outings, I make a point worth making. What greatly moves me can move others. The best arguments are lived.

* * *

The sun is high in the trees now, casting its first beams of light into the clearing. Blue jay calling. Murmur of the stream echoing through the forest. Red maple leaves glowing against an azure sky. The great calm persists. The wild is never more friendly than this. It'll be hard to leave it behind. On the other hand, I've gotten what I came for. Nothing matters quite so much now as simply being alive. I celebrate that quietly with each breath I take.

Late morning. Kaylee playing cards while I write. Just returned to camp after an early morning hike up Mt. Wilson. Spent a little time at the lookout. Kaylee's word for what can be seen there: *Amazing!* She wanted to call her mom and tell her about it but the cell service wasn't there. Clouds moving in now. We'll be breaking camp and hiking down to the New Haven River soon for another night. With any luck, it won't be as damp there.

* * *

Kaylee just got phone service. Talking to her mom now. It's a brave new world.

Late evening. Matika snuggled in close to me – more for the foam pad than affection. The moon has risen. It's half full. The campfire is dying down. There's a loon on the lake. It called out right before dinnertime, but is quiet now. The air is still so an incredible silence pervades. One has to experience this to believe it. I am *listening* to the fire. That and the breathing of myself and Matika.

It's hard to believe that I'm actually here. I expect to awaken from this dream any second now. But no, everything is too vivid, including Matika's sudden snoring. So much for silence.

• • •

Spiritual teachers talk about mindfulness, the importance of it and how difficult it is to achieve. Yet out here, sitting for a day, it becomes irresistible. That's why I'm here.

* * *

Beaver lodge half-hidden in the reeds. More goes on here than one might think.

* * *

Details, details. We clutter our lives with so many details that we forget to live. But here at this deep forest lake an elemental simplicity reigns. If I stop moving long enough, I can reap its rewards, relearn how to be.

* * *

I come out here to think because here I'm not so easily distracted. The trees make no advertisements. They simply are. And the jay calling in the distance invites me to do the same. Good, wild, real.

* * *

If God doesn't live in these forested mountains, than it can't be more than a figment of my imagination. In this deep silence, existence speaks to me loud and clear.

* * *

It took two days, but eventually the loon called out and made me cry…

Existential tears. Adam suddenly realizing that he has been cast out of paradise forever. Here, in the wild, so very close to regaining it.

83

Pillsbury Lake, Adirondacks

Late afternoon. I'm lost in a series of daydreams as long as the shadows cast by trees across the forest floor. A nearby loon calls out and I awaken from one reverie only to slip into another. I am intoxicated by the smell of the balsams standing tall all around me.

* * *

To meditate is simply to take a break from both the future and the past.

* * *

Pink follows orange across the sky until both colors concentrate on the western horizon – brightest half an hour after dusk. Then the liminal edge of night advancing like visible time, until the stars come out.

Evening. Just before dusk. Have adjusted the tarp lower so that its highest point is only two feet off the ground. Am using my woodpile as a barrier against the wind. It's blowing harder now. Matika looks concerned. Dry leaves blowing all over the place so having a fire was very dangerous. I built one just big enough to boil up water for ramen noodles, then snuffed it out. Matika comes over for snugs and reassurance. We'll get under the tarp soon. Camp all squared away but I won't get under the tarp until I have to. Should've brought my tent.

* * *

I forgot how helpless I feel when the wind blows hard enough through the mountains. Helpless and small.

* * *

Half buried in dry leaves. Someday I'll laugh about it.

Rung the sweat from my bandana during a short break an hour into the woods. Matika up to her belly in muck already, having slipped off the old puncheon crossing a cedar bog. A thrush chirping alarm as we pass by. And so it begins.

* * *

Popped ibuprofen while getting out of bed. I'm the Tin Man in desperate need of a lube.

* * *

Backpacking keeps me humble, despite the brag of it.

* * *

 Desperate thinking. When you're tired, depressed and feeling desperate, the whole world looks dark. Not a good time to make an important decision.

* * *

Tinker, a hiker five months on the Appalachian Trail, looked like a wild animal. Approached camp that way, too.

Sometimes I can't tell if this woods life is a dream or if my other life is. Seems impossible that they could both be real.

* * *

Ate the entire dehydrated meal (beef stew) and glad I did. 500 calories. Matika licked the container clean. Dinner's done. Better clean up, pump water, and get under the net before the bugs eat me alive.

* * *

Impossible to register all the sights and sounds out here, much less record them.

* * *

Matika wolfs down her lunch. Literally.

* * *

Signs of moose and coyote for days. Matika has noticed, too.

* * *

Flecks of mica in the gray sand of the spring look like gold. A precious place.

This morning is a turning point in more ways than one. Finishing the trail's meandering "U" with Mud Pond being its easternmost point. Now I move steadily south and/or west towards Monson. Also a personal "turning" from a wilderness visitor to a woodswalker. Have settled into being out here now.

* * *

Everyone has their own reasons for being out here. The only thing we share: a love of the woods.

* * *

There is a disproportionate number of thru hikers on this section of the Appalachian Trail, and many of them are about to finish. I want to congratulate them, but the truth is their approach to the trail is the opposite of mine. I'm more of a stop and smell the roses kind of guy. They have their eyes on the prize, although most will tell you that isn't their primary reason for being out here.

* * *

Everyone has their own pace. Everyone has their own goal. It's pointless to try to determine which is better. In this regard, I part with Thoreau and all other moralists. This much is certain: the final destination for

88

all of us is the grave, so unless you really want to create an impressive and lasting obituary, the journey itself is all that matters. Yes, the journey – life is a passing through this world. Make the most of it.

* * *

Another beautiful day. There's been a string of them lately. I feel quite fortunate to be out here right now. Few bugs, cool temps, sunny sky. A good day for daydreaming down the trail.

* * *

Fording and dread. Rarely is the anticipated threat as great as the one that sneaks up on you.

* * *

Woods Wanderer, I call myself, because it's the hardest thing in the world for me to stay on the trail.

* * *

I figure there are three types of visitors to the wild: 1) those who see it and run away, 2) those who are oblivious to it, 3) those who find a part of themselves in it. Yes, strangely familiar… as if, on some other plane of existence, a part of oneself never leaves the woods.

89

Quarter moon over the pond, to remind me that there are other worlds out there.

* * *

At North Pond I finally felt it: the dread of leaving the wild.

Among the trees. The sound of the brook, the wave of limbs over head, and cool air to breathe. The forest smells clean to me.

* * *

Being here makes more sense than being home and writing about it.

Makita and I are sitting in the shade of hemlocks right now, eating lunch. Nothing but blue sky overhead. Preston Brook is full of runoff and roaring just below us. A chickadee nearby. The forest is awash with light.

Whoa! Two deer just appeared behind us. Got within ten yards before spotting Matika. She gave chase without giving it a thought. I called after her immediately, so she stopped in her tracks twenty yards away then came back to me. Good dog! That was fun. Looks like we aren't the only ones enjoying this beautiful spring day.

* * *

Sometimes, when I'm indoors and feeling detached from the world, my "naturalist" pretensions seem ridiculous to me. But one thing's for certain: I am a woods wanderer pure and simple. I am at home here.

I love the woods – the green chaos of it. The mossy rocks, downed branches and trees, the upward struggle of living plants towards sunlight, the shadows, the ferns, the thick forest duff. Most of all, I love the smell of it. Clean rot. Wild purity. And the faint perfume of half-hidden wildflowers. Who needs heaven when there's a wild forest to roam?

* * *

The snap of a twig, the rustle of dead leaves… Matika's ears up and her nose twitching. And I am reaching for the camera in my pocket, as if it was a sidearm.

* * *

Blue smoke from the campfire hanging in the trees, slowly dissipating. My presence in the world is that ephemeral.

* * *

To be fair, there are moments in the lowlands that I enjoy almost as much as these woods. Almost.

Met John at 7:30 a.m. after a two-hour drive. Left his car at Sherburne Pass around 8-ish. Then we drove to Norwich in mine. Good hike today. Love my new pack. Talked too much, per usual. All excited to see John. A few great views, clear into New Hampshire. Very tired right now but I expect to rally in the morning. I'm into this.

* * *

"Grueling" is the word that comes to mind when thinking about today's hike, though I was somewhat entertained by the meander through both meadows and woods. Went through several pastures with cows in them. Interesting. Different.

* * *

On the trail by 8, finished by 3:30. Short day. Did ten miles but it seemed relatively easy compared to Sunday and Monday. I talked my way uphill in the morning – poor John – and drank plenty of water. Good night's sleep last night. That helped.

Noon. I'm camped out beneath a poplar along the edge of a parking lot, watching traffic race by. John is slack-packing the last two miles to Sherburne Pass. Over half of his stuff is next to me, beneath a plastic sheet, so he should be traveling fast. Time is of the essence. We need to finish today's hike, go get my car in Norwich, then shuttle him to Highway 30 just outside Manchester with enough time left for him to reach a shelter before dark. I'm off the trail.

* * *

Started hanging out at Thundering Falls, until John asked me to make a conscious choice to either stay or go. With time a concern, I opted to go. I honestly believe he would have lingered there if I had wanted to.

95

Despite fatigue, bugs and dampness, it's good to be out here. The drive was telltale: interstate, then highway, then dirt road, then one-lane track. And then walking the footpath. And then bushwhacking. The gradual immersion into wildness. Much like getting comfortable. The structures and formalities stripped away.

* * *

Earth, sky, rushing water, still forest. The only things that make sense to me.

* * *

Nature was Thoreau's mistress. The wild is mine.

Beneath the tarp (and bug net), taking a break from the black flies after setting up camp. Early evening and it's still warm and sunny. Will start a fire and cook dinner soon, when it cools down a bit and the flies go away. They've already taken enough of my blood.

* * *

Slabsides is a much more "rustic" cabin than I expected it to be. And curiously perched on the edge of a celery swamp. A peaceful place, no doubt good for John Burroughs's writing and study. Yet no more a wilderness retreat than Thoreau's camp on Walden. The ghost of Burroughs was there, somewhat, but I feel a greater presence in these mountains. Perhaps I'm wrong, but I think he had more wildness in him than Slabsides could accommodate.

* * *

Sunlight filtering through the tops of the trees overhead as the sun crests the distant ridge. How can anyone be godless on a morning like this?

A *very* damp forest. Deer flies menacing on the trail, otherwise an easy hike in here. I enjoyed it despite the minor miseries. Traveling light and using trekking poles. Feel like my old self again. It takes deep woods to do it. I haven't felt this good in years – mentally, that is. Getting past the physical hardships, of course.

* * *

Matika chews a stick. I whittle a piece of wood into a spoon. Not much difference.

* * *

A pair of loons swim near shore. By the time I fetch my camera, they are gone. Ephemeral wildness.

* * *

Unpredictable sky encouraging me to just go with the flow. That's the kind of day it is.

* * *

Wind whispering through the conifers. Listening to it is a form of meditation.

If I spent a week on a lake like this, could I plumb the philosophical depths of wildness the way I'd like to, or would I simply daydream?   What's the difference between the two?

* * *

Doing a lot of nothing today, and not finished yet.

* * *

The fertile forest is both a nursery and a graveyard. Upon close inspection, the cycle of life is appalling. We civilized folk keep it all so contained.

* * *

All the world is nature. The folly of humankind is in thinking we live beyond it.

* * *

The sights, sounds and smells of the forest are reason enough to live.

* * *

Our lives consist of the choices we make. There is no one else to blame.

Matika startled by a raven that swooped overhead and started croaking loudly just after dusk. Remembering my time in Alaska, I took the visit as a good omen.

* * *

Never sharpen your knife in the streets of a city, and never count your money in the woods.

* * *

Up at six. Down with the sun last night. Didn't sleep all that time, but I awoke feeling the full effect of gravity. Heavy sleep, and strange dreams.

Remember well hiking back here many years ago on a walking meditation of sorts, and taking a nap next to the brook at a place not unlike this one. What do such meditations produce other than a deeper connection to the wild? A sense of perspective, perhaps. Not much else. I drop down on my knees and drink straight from the brook now as I did them. Not much has changed about me.   I remain the same woods wandering bushman I've always been.

Out here overnight with Matika, camped along the advancing edge of spring. Left the trail where it crosses the brook a second time, then bushwhacked to here – a good quarter mile upstream from my old campsite, which is now occupied by a colony of ants. No matter. Change is good.

* * *

Hermit thrush just after dusk, so far away it's almost as if I imagine it.

* * *

Who am I? Just a guy tossing pieces of wood on a campfire, somewhere in the Green Mountains in early spring. Everything else is window dressing.

* * *

Water bugs skimming the surface of the brook while I splash water into my face then pump enough to drink. Matika chewing on a stick already, patiently awaiting breakfast. My first thought this morning: It gets harder to be out here as I grow older, but is more rewarding.

How easy it is to forget the Real, even when you have an idea of it. The senses must be awakened to it.

* * *

If I become too didactic while preaching about the wild, the gist of it will be lost. Keep the soul in it no matter what.

* * *

The soul is manifest in the senses. We are animals still.

* * *

The campfire snaps and crackles. The orange flames dance. The embers beneath the charred sticks glow. Ah, the smell of it! The smell of deep forest freedom. Just now a gentle breeze fans the fire until it burns smoke free. The warmth of it is reassuring. I am never completely lost in the world as long as I have a small circle of stones and a fire within.

103

When I am alone in the woods, off trail and soaked with rainwater and sweat, I am completely at home in the world.

* * *

I am a woods wanderer to be sure. Where do I begin and the forest end?

* * *

It must have rained hard last night. The forest is brilliant green, and the forest floor is covered with foamflower – a favorite wildflower of mine. Also miterwort, yellow clintonia, wild ginseng, twinflower, violets, and Canada mayflower. But today it's all about foamflower, and I love it. I love these wet, wild woods and everything in it. I love the bugs, moss, blowdown, ferns, songbirds and all the rest. Or is this just the ozone talking? I am intoxicated by the forest.

A spider crawls across my thigh and I quickly knock it away. And for a split second I am keenly aware of all the bugs and microbes surrounding me. Much more terrifying than a bear or any other predator. If I died in these woods, the wild would quickly consume me.

* * *

What I like most about the wild forest is how living and dying take place with such ease, blended together, seamless. This is my definition of eternity. Even the rocks compress, then break down. Permanence is an illusion.

* * *

Nature is all there is. Wildness is the purest expression of it, devoid of the human illusion of separateness. We move chemical configurations around and then say: "Look! We are gods!" But neither the rock slowly eroding nor the stream breaking a path downhill is much impressed. And the wind knows better.

Matika and I have stopped for lunch after bushwhacking a mile back from the dirt road. My snowshoes have come in handy, at long last. I've been floating on top of a foot of the white stuff. Sometimes more. Followed bobcat tracks for a while. A partly cloudy day with temps in the 20s. More late winter than early spring. The brook murmurs beneath the snow. A few glimpses of it here and there, but mostly covered over. Just now a cold wind making the trees creak. Matika spots a squirrel. Are those turkey tracks? A woodpecker pecks at a dead tree otherwise all is quiet. Good to be out here breathing fresh air and breaking a sweat in the woods, but I wish the snow were gone. It's been a long, hard winter.

* * *

Hemlock cones atop the snow. Regeneration.

Rising from the water after a quick dunk, I raise my closed eyes to the sun and feel the warm air and icy droplets mix on my skin. A moment of pagan joy.

* * *

Pensive before the dunk and now afterward. Hard to explain why. Flux, natural beauty, stillness, and the passage of time. And mute awe in the face of the ineffable. Order and chaos: right here, right now.

After throwing a line in North Pond to no avail, we hiked back to the campground, walked out to the narrows of May Pond, and got into sunfish and perch there. Caught and released about thirty between us, sometimes fishing in the rain. Came back to camp for a potpourri dinner and a blazing campfire. Did that despite the drizzle. Inside the tent now, Matika wet and dirty next to me, and snoring. Mason and Hunter playing cards and telling stories. I'm pooped and just about to fall asleep. Carrying a bundle of firewood (along with a full pack) took something out of me. The boys are wide awake.

I have plenty of work to do back home but Judy urged me to seize the day and go into the woods overnight by myself. She said I need it. She usually knows before I do. It didn't take much convincing. I gathered up food and gear and was out the door by 10:30. Now here I am, lounging in the woods. In my element. Not enough of this. Long overdue, actually. The brook convinces me of it, as does the forest silence.

* * *

The campfire burns away my concerns…

* * *

Nothing more humbling than to be a man of the woods. The elements reduce me.

* * *

Moonlight or sunlight – mottled forest, light and dark. Endlessly layered, textured, deep.

* * *

I know nothing about God, nature, or the world at large except what the elements teach me.

* * *

Fire, water, earth and sky. The elements diminish my ego to practically nothing, then rebuild it in the image of wild nature. I am the elements. They are me. And any pretense to the contrary is gone.

* * *

Politics, religion and the modern world. The older I get, the more hopeless it all seems – beyond any meaningful reform. All I can do is embrace the wild and live my life the best I can.

Judy and I have stolen into the woods for an overnighter, taking advantage of an unusual run of warm, sunny days following the first hard frost. Indian Summer, or something like it. With temps hitting 80 degrees today, more like a summer extension, although golden leaves in the trees above us tell us otherwise. A beautiful day to sit next to a mountain brook and enjoy the forest all the same.

* * *

Judy knitting while sitting against a tree, six feet from the fire. She looks pensive.

* * *

"What's it all for?" Judy asks as we stare into the campfire, after dinner, once it's completely dark. She's questioning the meaning of all existence. Music to my ears! I do my best to keep an exchange of ideas going, but eventually I'm on a rant about God, the evolution of the universe, and the efficacy of wild nature. Judy says "So what?" to it all. She makes a good point with that, a point that any existentialist would endorse. The only meaning we have, it seems, is that which we create.

And yet I still believe in an order to the universe called nature, and in a God that created it. Go figure.

* * *

Judy embraces the Buddhist belief in the impermanence of all things. Sounds like Heraclitus to me. Flux. Spinoza. A gateway to pantheism?

* * *

No one knows the mind of God. I'm not the first person to say this.

* * *

Truth. Love. Beauty. Nature. By themselves these words seem trite, as they do in all abstract discussions. And yet the Real screams them into the world.

* * *

Judy notices horsetail for the first time. I point out fungus, moss, ferns and club moss, and suddenly we are immersed in a very old world. We and the flowering plants are newcomers.

* * *

Keeping a campfire going long after breakfast for no other reason than to have a focus for our attention, we resume the previous evening's philosophizing. Somehow it is less terrifying by the light of day, and we are more rational.

* * *

A few birds chirping, otherwise the forest is still. Meister Eckhart said nothing is more like God than stillness.

* * *

There's an old dead tree leaning towards our camp. Eventually, it will make this spot uninhabitable. The pool across the brook, once a favorite place to go for a dunk, has dried up thanks to a diverted and ever-changing stream. Nothing stays the same.

* * *

Judy comes out here to gain perspective by getting away. I, on the other hand, am doing a reality check. Wild nature orients us both.

* * *

Water over stone on its way to the sea… The incessant rush of water, washing my thoughts into oblivion.

* * *

Over lunch Judy and I remembering previous visits here, and elsewhere in the woods – all too aware of the passage of time.

The stream, translucent before me, turns into the roily, muddy, bank-full Lamoille River not too far below. Much rain after a relatively dry May. I welcome it.

* * *

When I move, the forest stands still. When I stand still, the forest moves.

The rotting remnant of a tree, all covered with moss and cobwebs and fungus, surrounded by young green plants asserting themselves, reminds me of nature's incredible bounty, as well as its chaos and decay – all wrapped up together.   And I am a part of it.   And I too will be recycled someday.

* * *

The sun slips beneath the trees and the slow sigh towards darkness begins.   Evening, when it's time to reflect.   Now the campfire commands my attention, becomes the center of my universe.   Blow three times on it and watch it come alive.

* * *

Matika watches intently while I feed the campfire.   I wonder what she's thinking.

* * *

Wetter wood burns slow and smoky, much like dull minds.

I am intimidated by the incessant flow of the mountain stream, knowing that it will continue flowing long after I'm gone, carrying away bits of me into oblivion. And yet there is consolation in that as well. Someday I too will be ever-flowing.

Camped at the headwaters of the New Haven River – the exact same place where I camped ten days ago. This time I have Judy with me, and a whole lot more stuff, including a tent too big for the site. But the sun is shining through the green canopy, the stream is running clear, and the temps are just about ideal, so we are happy to be here for the next couple days. A true holiday in the woods.

* * *

The fire burns hottest when there is just the right amount of space between the pieces of wood. Fire loves company, but doesn't want to be crowded.

* * *

I find the joy of these wilderness outings to be transient. If I were to build a cabin on this spot, much of this woody delight would be retained, but something would be lost in the process. The less impact I have, the more wildness seeps into me.

* * *

There are so many small creatures eating away at the deadfall that it's surprising we can't hear constant munching.

* * *

You can't fish a brook properly without getting your feet wet.

* * *

A few of those black and white butterflies linger in camp. At midday dozens of them had gathered here, drawn to our wet, dirty clothes on the clothesline, but also to our tent and other gear. I saw plenty more while fishing this morning. They are abundant along this stream, and quite beautiful upon close inspection.

* * *

More blowdown, washouts and mudslides along this brook than I recall. Makes me think of climate change. Anyone who has spent a lifetime in these woods can see it. Believing it is another thing, of course.

* * *

119

The forest makes me deeply religious, because only here is it evident that there is more to the world than what I, or any of my kind, can create or manipulate.

Mid-afternoon. Eating a late lunch after partially setting up camp. There's a large, beautiful pool a couple hundred feet away, fed by a small waterfall. When I stumbled upon it, I decided to make this my home for the night.

. . .

The pool is even bigger up close. About thirty feet square and chest deep. I know because I went in. Matika waded up to her belly along the edge. Good enough.

* * *

A barred owl ushers in the night.

* * *

(Screech?) owl loud and clear in the wee hours. Matika suddenly on guard.

* * *

Life is too short to wasted having regrets. Each day dawns entirely new. Have another go at it.

Good to be on the woods again: simple, solitary, organic, and earthbound. Good to cut through the illusions of modern living. Good to be natural for a while.

The stream rushes along. The sweet, earthy smell of the late-summer forest intoxicates me. Mosquitoes for company – just so that that I don't get too comfortable. It's all good. I'd rather be here than in the finest hotel. This suits me better.

* * *

So many people afraid of bears… Thank god! Otherwise there would be no forest solitude.

* * *

"No Camping" sign at the trailhead parking lot. Is that really necessary? Maybe it is. Maybe it's against the rules for me to be here right now. I'll have to look into that someday.

* * *

If I push over a tree so that it falls in the forest, does anyone else care? Does anyone else hear it?

* * *

If God is not in these trees all around me, then he doesn't exist. Hence my reluctant pantheism.

* * *

Death is not nearly as terrifying as the prospect of a life not fully lived.

* * *

Comfort is relative. Happiness is an attitude. Life is short.

Hunter, Mason and I are now in the tent, retired for the evening. The boys are goofin' on each other while I write this. We're camped on the south shore of the pond, after learning the hard way the north shore trail to the tenting site has been closed. Surprise, surprise. With my legs cramping up, I found this relatively flat spot in the hobblebush and declared it home for the night. All three of us were exhausted after a long tramp over Stratton Mountain and to this pond. The last mile was the hardest. "The trail of doom," as Mason dubbed it.

* * *

Mason giddy at dinnertime, eating his ramen noodles. "I can't believe we're doing this!"

* * *

Silence. Incredibly quiet here at the pond. No wind. No owls. Nothing but the occasional murmur of backpackers on the other side of the pond.

* * *

Owl at midnight. Loon at dawn, along with chattering chipmunks. The still pond is dappled with insect activity. The sun shines over the low ridge in the distance that rises to Stratton Mountain. An absolutely picture perfect day. This is why I come out here.

* * *

Time for breakfast. It'll be interesting to see how the boys react to this morning.

Another great day on the Appalachian Trail with John. We got a good early start from Stratton Pond and crossed Windhall River shortly thereafter. Stopped there to admire the tannic stream flowing then talked to a southbound AT thru hiker. Overcast, cool, dripping forest most of the day. The occasional thru hiker encountered. No one else. Disoriented by a new road just outside my beloved Lye Brook Wilderness. Wasn't there in '95 when I passed thru here. Prospect Rock a real treat. John and I hung out there a while eating lunch. Fog rolled in over Manchester, Vermont below. Very cool. Talked and walked all the way to Spruce Peak Shelter, getting there around 1 p.m. Decided to go for the highway. Out of the woods 2:30.

* * *

Shuttled down to Dalton, Massachusetts to flip John – get him back on the trail headed north.

* * *

Stinky, dirty, sore, tired, chilled at times, wet, underfed, and happy to be here.

If everyone knew what a pleasure it is to sit by a brook, feeding sticks into a campfire at dusk, with only a dog for company, it would be almost impossible to be alone in the woods.

* * *

Wildness and being human. I suppose it is possible to be fully human in an artificial environment, completely divorced from nature, but I can't imagine it.

* * *

The universe is a curious mix of order and chaos. What better illustration of this than the trees in a forest – the way they grow, compete for light and soil, decay and recycle in the endlessly branched world in which they live?

First things I did upon arriving here were to put four large stones back into the fire pit (why were they in the shelter?), wipe down my dog, then use the same towel to wipe out the shelter (no broom here). Then I slung a line for my wet clothes and set up the mosquito bar. The mosquitoes aren't bad yet, but I expect them to be. I also checked out the obvious access to the water, stumbled upon a hornets' nest there and took two hits. Haven't found a good alternative access to the water yet. Will do that soon.

* * *

Is this Matika's last big adventure? I'm afraid so. Old girl is pushing twelve, and those hips are a problem. I'll enjoy her company while I can.

* * *

I came out here to contemplate the relationship between God, man and nature, and see if my outdoor thoughts match my indoor ones. But right now that seems like a bad idea. Right now it seems more important to simply be here. Hard to say why. Because nature has no opinions, no philosophy or religion. It just is.

Mist on the opposite shore. The lake perfectly still. A grey, formless sky. Thick vegetation around camp. Packed earth immediately around the shelter. They say each tablespoon of rich forest soil contains six billion microbes. Egads!

* * *

Love of truth? That's why I call myself a philosopher. Love of nature? Tell me in what way is truth and nature different. Any philosopher who doesn't come ultimately to nature is a charlatan, I'm convinced. Reality is wildness, first and foremost.

* * *

I say I'm a lover of truth, but the truth is I'm just afraid of it as the next guy. The foremost truth is: I'm going to die someday, and knowing that, with absolute certainty *before* the fact, is what sets me apart from the rest of the animal kingdom – from all nature, actually.

* * *

Nature, what it is exactly, is the greatest of all mysteries. We are doomed to live our lives utterly oblivious to it, despite all our gray matter. Science is, at best, an approximation of the Real. After all, we cannot know the absolute truth about nature without knowing how/why it came to be.

* * *

Tell me that I have always been at this lake, and a part of me will believe you – the part of me that always lives in the now.

* * *

Loon calls out, late afternoon, just to remind me where I am.

* * *

Why all these dead spruces around the shelter? Do I dare inquire?

* * *

We see ourselves reflected in nature because we *are* nature – a part of it, anyhow. Whatever we say about nature, we say about ourselves. Whatever we say about ourselves, we say about nature. To commune with nature is simply to go back to the source and remember who/what we are.

Homo faber. Toolmakers we are, no doubt, but that's not all we are. There is more to creativity than innovation. And our wild minds enable us to see nature as no other creature can, to appreciate her and not just use her.

* * *

A beautiful spider's web high in the trees. Spiders are not my favorite creatures, but you have to admire their work. How did they learn that symmetry?

* * *

While gathering wood, I find a downed conifer with ideal branches sticking up – neither green nor rotten. The branches snap off nicely. The bark twists off easily. Good firewood. Then I notice all the activity on the main trunk: three types of fungus, two types of moss, and lichen doing their best to break down the remnant tree. Insects doing their part, no doubt, along with all kinds of bacteria. The forest engine. The cycle of life. Dynamic biomass everywhere all around me. "Nothing in wilderness escapes universal inter-dependence," John Hay wrote in *The Immortal Wilderness.* That is obvious to anyone who comes out here. A mosquito lands on my arm and I wonder how many there are out here. Probably best if I don't know. But the blood they take from me and other creatures feeds the forest engine. It all connects. And yet no one player is indispensible. The web of life, long before the Internet yet operating the same way. Phenomenal, really. Everywhere I look, growth and decay. And me right in the middle of it.

* * *

Ralph Waldo Emerson said: "We can love nothing but nature." Now *that* makes me scratch my head! I think I know what he means, and I agree in principle, but I'm not sure that "we," all of humankind, could ever embrace that worldview.

* * *

Every excursion alone into the wild is a spiritual undertaking. That's the way it feels to me, anyhow. God, "the Eternal Thou" as Martin Buber puts it, is manifest in nature. Of that I am certain.

* * *

Dancing lid on a pot of boiling water. How much of animation is only heat and water?

* * *

Nature: the whole being greater than the sum of its parts.

* * *

The spider's web near my camp is best seen from an angle. Head on, it disappears. So it is with any approach to Nature – nature with a capital "N" that is, the philosopher's nature.

* * *

Reproduction, ingestion, growth – what is it all *for*? Some people tell me that it is *for* nothing really, it just *is*. But that doesn't satisfy me. In a cosmos that sprung from a singularity to superheated plasma, to fiery stars, what need is there for life at all? It seems superfluous in an inanimate universe. It seems… freakish.

* * *

Either the universe is organized according to some principle, or everything is random. The latter is difficult to believe.

* * *

God does not exist any more or less than Nature does.

Evolution, what a concept. I'm convinced that it is the first, the last, the only real miracle in the universe. I'm convinced that it is the only real proof we have of the existence of God.

* * *

Yes, absolutely, I see woody chaos whenever I tramp through the forest. But look closely and you will see whorled leaves, symmetry, and intricate patterns in flowers. Growth and decay. Order and chaos. It's all there.

* * *

Butterfly on my thigh. Day four. "What did you do?" they'll ask me. But it's not what I did, but what the butterfly did.

* * *

Does the world belong to insects or bacteria? Take your pick. Not mammals. Not me. I can destroy the world but I cannot possess it.

* * *

An inchworm floating down to land on my finger.

One of the hardest things to do is to be quiet, still, and entertain one's thoughts while immersed in wildness. It's terrifying, really. The mind recoils from it, afraid of what might surface. The fear of wildness is primal. It is the fear of the unknown. We are afraid, first and foremost, of what we were *before* we were civilized. We imagine the worst. But letting go of all that, it becomes incredibly easy and natural to simply be in the moment. I find myself laughing at the absurdity of my self-image, my sense of self-importance: MAN. When a butterfly lands on me, I am only a perch.

* * *

Humankind has a tendency to put things in boxes, categories. I am no exception to this. I talk about my mind, body and soul as if they are separate things. I talk about God, man and nature as if they are entirely separate entities. We assume that the physical and the spiritual are completely different realms. And that's how our thoughts become muddled, out of sync with reality.

* * *

Does Nature will itself? Is the apparent order that we perceive in Nature an extension of the *mind* of Nature? Are our minds a part of that mind? Is chemistry just another word for spirit? Clearly there is more that we

136

don't know than there is that we do know when we go down this path, but down it we go to understand the whole. Otherwise our understanding of Nature, and consequently ourselves, is only a collection of pieces.

* * *

When it comes to truth, the only heresy is that which forces us to stop asking questions.

* * *

The incredible universe, the miracle of life, the great mystery of nature, this phenomenon called man – it all presses reason to its limit and beyond. I call myself a philosopher, but there are times when the term "mystic" would be more appropriate. When pressed to it, I cannot explain Nature. I can only marvel at it.

* * *

While fetching water for dinner, I splash a little of the lake into my face then raise my closed eyes to the sky before opening them to a brightly shining sun. Call it a prayer.

* * *

Dusk. My first campfire, a couple of days ago, was to keep up my skills and save fuel. The second one, last night, was for pleasure. This one is religion.

* * *

"Whoa!" I say when a light suddenly shines in my face, then a second one. Matika barks. Two young men appear so we go out to meet them.

* * *

The spell has been broken. Now that I have company, the deep solitude has passed. Suddenly I'm feeling like breaking camp and heading out early.

* * *

Have decided to make a little campfire this morning, just to slow myself down. Besides, Todd and Phil might like it. It'll keep the bugs down. A farewell fire.

* * *

So now it's late morning. My gear is organized and ready to pack. The fire is out. It's time to go.

About the Author

Walt McLaughlin received a degree in philosophy from Ohio University in 1977 and has been wondering, wandering and writing ever since. He has over a dozen books in print, including a narrative about his immersion in the Alaskan bush, *Arguing with the Wind*, and one about backpacking through the Adirondacks, *The Allure of Deep Woods*. He is also the force behind a small press called Wood Thrush Books, and has selected and published the works of several 19th Century writers including *The Laws of Nature: Excerpts from the Writings of Ralph Waldo Emerson*. He lives in Swanton, Vermont with his wife, Judy.

For more information about Walt's books, visit the WTB website: **www.woodthrushbooks.com**

Go to **www.facebook.com\WaltMcLaughlin** to check out his Facebook page, or read his regularly posted blogs at **www.woodswanderer.com**